ELLA
QUEEN OF
JAZZ

HELEN
HANCOCKS

Frances Lincoln
Children's Books

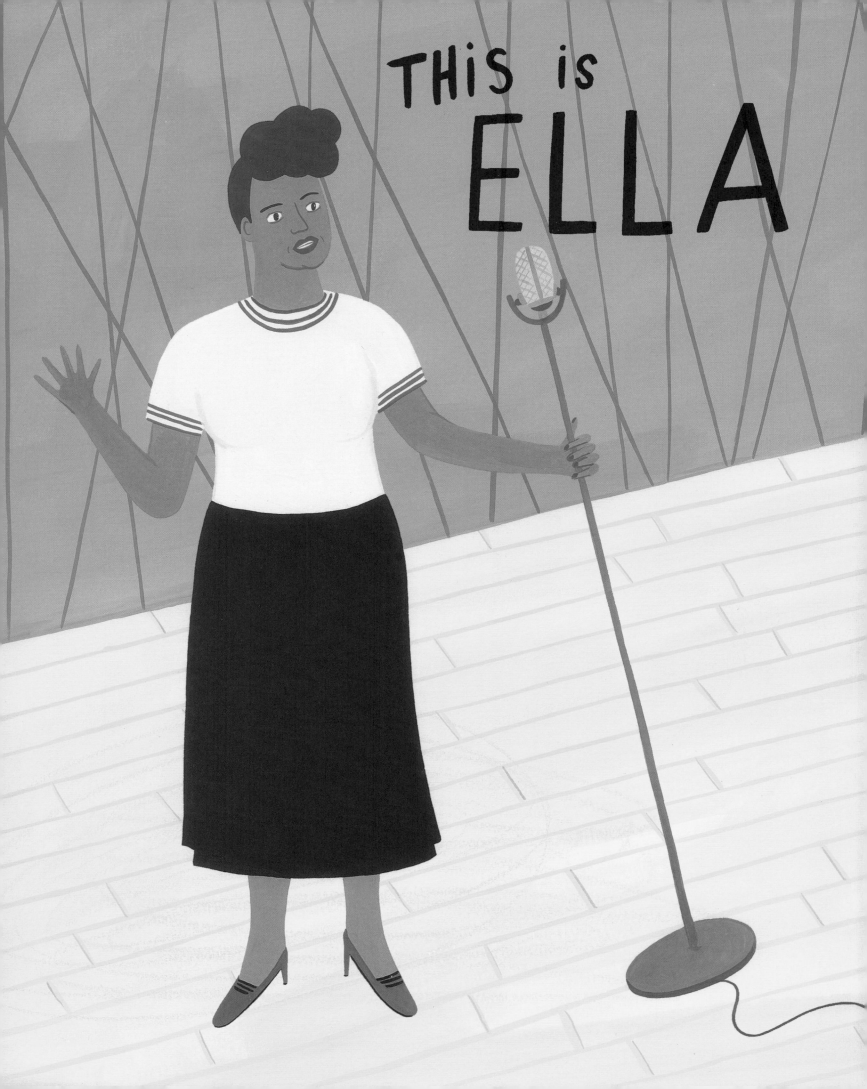

AND THESE ARE HER FELLAS.

Before long, Ella was taking
her music up and down the country.

It was a crazy time, and Ella was on her way up!

FOR ONE NIGHT ONLY!

* —ELLA—
FITZGERALD

* AND HER FELLAS *

But Ella and her band weren't welcome everywhere.

Ella was black, and some folks
didn't want her singing in their club...

"I'm sorry Ella, but the answer was no."

When Ella heard this news, it hit her hard.

"That's it, fellas," she said.
"Maybe we're not destined for the big time."

But the magic of Ella's music had
reached out to people all over,

and helped her to make friends she
    didn't even know she had, including one very special lady.

OFFICE

Ella's friend secretly decided to help.

"YOU MUST BOOK ELLA FITZGERALD, SHE WILL BE FABULOUS!"

"IF SHE PLAYS, I WILL SIT AT THE FRONT EVERY NIGHT FOR ALL THE PEOPLE AND PAPARAZZI IN TOWN TO SEE."

She could be pretty persuasive! Not long after, Ella had a call.

She and her fellas were asked to play the biggest joint in town – the very same one that had turned her away before.

And just as her friend had promised...

ELLA WAS
FABULOUS!

She was a hit with
the crowd.

And so was her friend!

"MARILYN MONROE, THIS ONE IS FOR YOU!"

With every night, the show got stronger and stronger,

and so did their friendship.

With all of Hollywood flocking to see them,

Marilyn and Ella discovered that a
little courage could go a long way.

As the saying goes, all good things come to an end,
and after a week, it was time for Ella's final show.

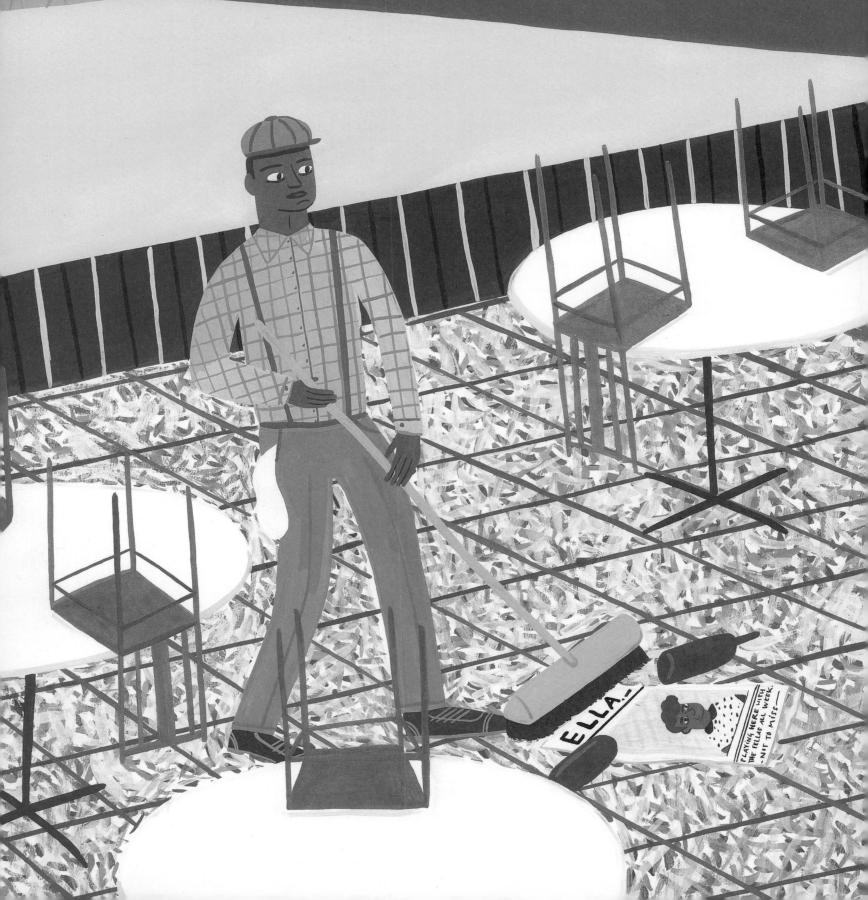

Ella felt sad.

But while the run might
have ended...

her friendship with Marilyn
certainly hadn't.

With a little help from her
friend, Marilyn Monroe went
on to become a great singer
in her own films.

She even sang for the president!

And Ella became known as the First Lady of Song –
the Queen of Jazz! – winning many awards along the way.

Just goes to show what friends can do for one another.

The End.

ELLA

Ella Fitzgerald, also known as the 'First Lady of Song', 'Queen of Jazz' or 'Lady Ella', was born 25 April 1917. Her childhood in Yonkers, New York, was hard and when she was just 15, her mother died. Ella danced on the streets of Harlem to earn money, which led her to perform at the Amateur Night at the Apollo Theatre. Because there was another dance act there, Ella decided to sing instead, and she won first prize.

This success pushed teenaged Ella in the direction of band leader and drummer Chick Webb, and around 1935 she joined his band. When he died in 1939, Ella became band leader and the band was renamed 'Ella and her Famous Orchestra'. They recorded nearly 150 songs together before Ella left in 1942 to focus on her solo career.

Around this time, the sound of jazz started to change, and Ella's sound changed, too. She added bebop and scat to her repertoire and came to be considered one of the best voices in jazz.

The events in this book took place in the 1950s. Marilyn Monroe lobbied the owner of a major nightclub to book Ella to perform, and the two women became friends.

The First Lady of Song released over 200 albums during her lifetime. Her appearances in films and on TV made her a household name and her songs garnered many awards, including 13 Grammys.

Ella died on 15 June 1996 aged 79, but her songs live on.

MARILYN

Marilyn Monroe was born Norma Jeane Mortenson on 1 June 1926. She was a model and actress and became an icon of her age.

Marilyn grew up in Los Angeles, California, and spent most of her childhood in foster homes and orphanages. She had a troubled private life as an adult, too, and married for the first time aged just 16. She got married two more times before she was 31 – to baseball player Joe DiMaggio and playwright Arthur Miller – but all of her marriages ended in divorce.

In 1944, Marilyn began modelling after she was photographed working in a factory during the Second World War. This led to minor roles in Hollywood films, and over the next couple of years she became one of the most bankable Hollywood stars with leading roles in films like *Gentleman Prefer Blondes*, *Bus Stop*, *Niagara* and *Some Like it Hot* (which won her a Golden Globe).

Although she was often typecast as the 'dumb blonde', Marilyn was actually very smart. She founded her own production company and studied method acting at the world-famous Actors Studio in New York City. One of her most iconic roles was in Billy Wilder's *The Seven Year Itch*. The last film she completed was John Huston's *The Misfits* in 1961, written by her third husband, Arthur Miller.

Marilyn died on 5 August 1962 aged just 36, yet she remains one of Hollywood's most recognisable stars and icons.

For all the great friendships in life —H.H.

First published in Great Britain in 2017 by Frances Lincoln Children's Books.
74–77 White Lion Street, London N1 9PF, UK
QuartoKnows.com · Visit our blogs at QuartoKnows.com

Copyright © Helen Hancocks 2017

A catalogue record for this book is available from the British Library.

This book is not produced or licensed by the Ella Fitzgerald Foundation.

ISBN 978-1-84780-918-6

Illustrated in gouache

Published by Rachel Williams · Edited by Jenny Broom
Designed by Nicola Price · Production by Laura Grandi

Manufactured in Shenzhen China, RD052018

5 7 9 8 6 4